AF262761

THE LITTLE BOOK OF

OASIS

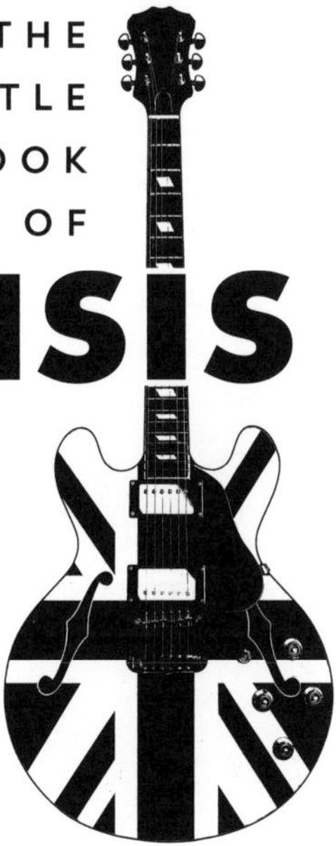

AN UNOFFICIAL CELEBRATION OF THE GREATEST ROCK 'N' ROLL BAND ON THE PLANET

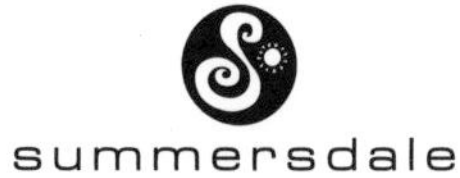

summersdale

THE LITTLE BOOK OF OASIS

Copyright © Octopus Publishing Group Limited, 2025

Text by Chris Turton

An Hachette UK Company
www.hachette.co.uk

Summersdale Publishers
Part of Octopus Publishing Group Limited
Carmelite House
50 Victoria Embankment
LONDON
EC4Y 0DZ
UK

www.summersdale.com

The authorized representative in the EEA is Hachette Ireland, 8 Castlecourt Centre, Dublin 15, D15 XTP3, Ireland (email: info@hbgi.ie)

Printed and bound in China

ISBN: 978-1-83799-720-6
eISBN: 978-1-83799-721-3

This FSC® label means that materials and other controlled sources used for the product have been responsibly sourced

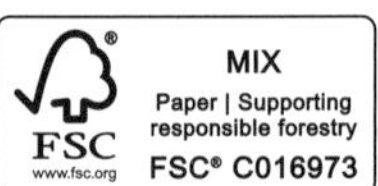

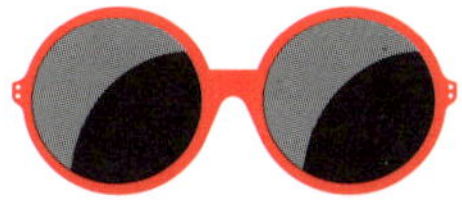

TO

....

FROM

....

INTRODUCTION

Are you ready to shake along with Oasis on a journey from their working-class roots to their supersonic breakthrough and beyond into the supernova of rock 'n' roll stardom?

This book paints a vivid picture of the phenomenal story behind one of the most talented, outrageous and controversial bands in history. It reveals candid facts about the undeniable personalities that make up the group and offers their uncensored, unfiltered opinions in their own words. If you think you know everything there is to know about Oasis, you can test your knowledge with the stack of trivia questions found throughout.

One thing is guaranteed – the notorious exploits of the Gallagher brothers and the band they assembled to make their mark and share their audacious, heartfelt message with the world will be anything but dull.

So, roll with it, take your time… and get mad fer it!

WE'RE NOT ARROGANT, WE JUST BELIEVE

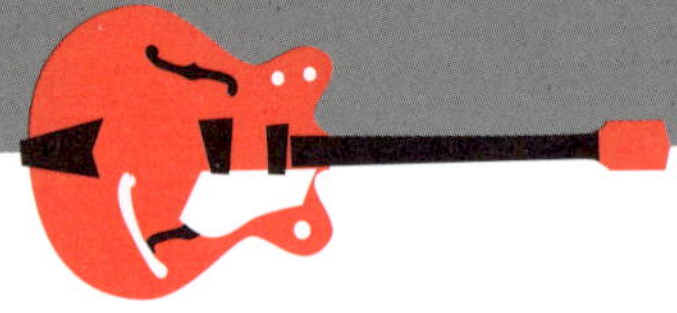

WE'RE THE BEST BAND IN THE WORLD.

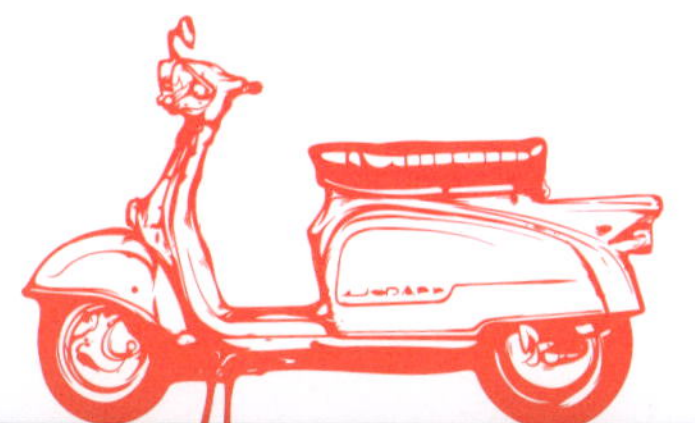

The band's name wasn't conceived in the middle of the Sahara or inspired by a fruity soft drink – it came from a venue listed on a gig poster for fellow Mancunian maestros Inspiral Carpets. They happened to be playing at the Oasis Leisure Centre in Swindon

In 1991, before Oasis were Oasis, Liam auditioned as a singer for a band featuring Paul McGuigan, Paul Arthurs and Tony McCarroll. What was this band's name?

---

a) **The Sunshine**

b) **The Rain**

c) **The Weathered**

I'M LIAM
GALLAGHER AND
I'M IN OASIS. THE
WHOLE WORLD IS
JEALOUS OF ME.
IT SHOULD BE.

LIAM

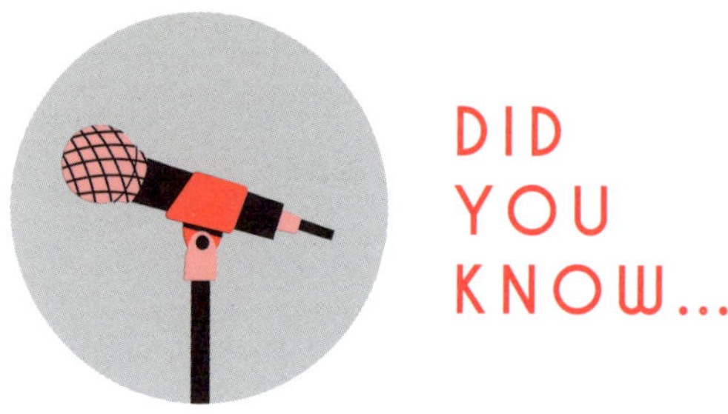

DID YOU KNOW...

In 1988, the Gallagher brothers attended a Stone Roses benefit gig at International 2, a venue located in their home city of Manchester. Liam and Noel have said that, were it not for that gig, they might never have decided to start a band.

Oasis made their UK television
debut on 18 March 1994
with a live performance of
"Supersonic". What show
did they perform on?

———

a) *Top of the Pops*

b) *TFI Friday*

c) *The Word*

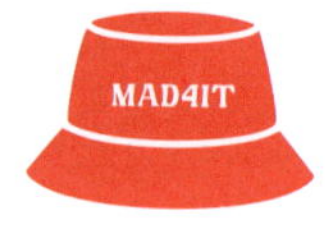

For me, the standout track is "Rock 'n' Roll Star"… coming from where we did, everyone dreamt of being a rock 'n' roll star.

BONEHEAD

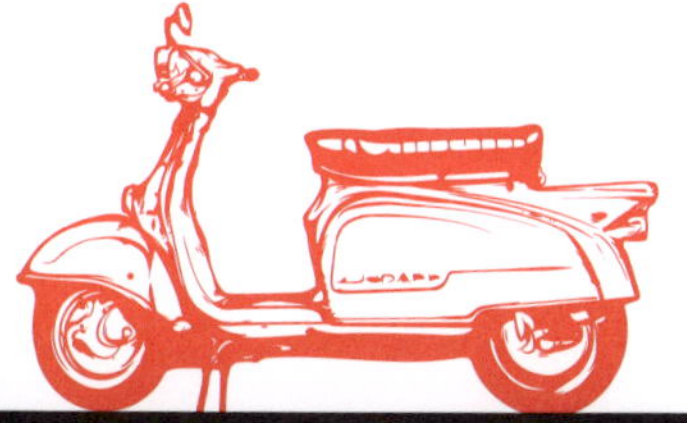

Liam is actually an abbreviation of William. His middle names are John and Paul, after (of course!) John Lennon and Paul McCartney. This is one of the many connections the band share with the Fab Four.

The band's first gig (which Noel went to see but did not play at) was in their hometown of Manchester, on the bill with the Catchmen and Sweet Jesus. What was the venue?

———

a) The Boardwalk

b) Band on the Wall

c) New Century

ROCK 'N' ROLL
TO ME IS ALL
ABOUT FREEDOM
OF THOUGHT,

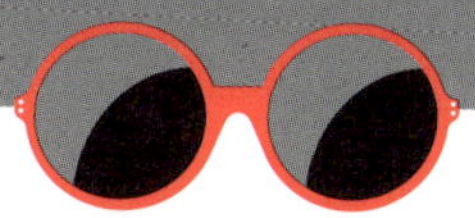

AND TO BE
WHATEVER YOU
WANT TO BE.

NOEL

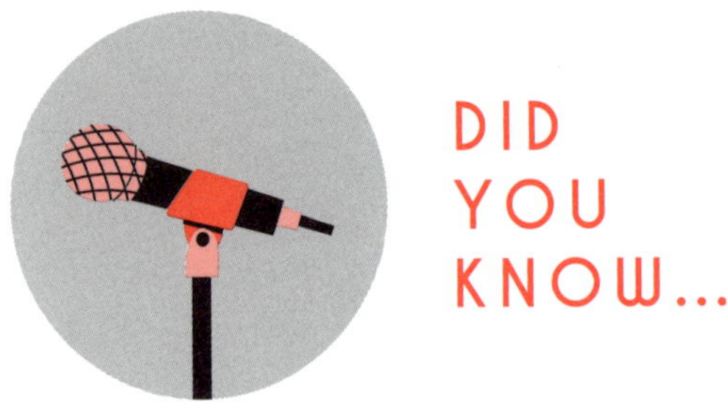

The iconic photograph used for the album cover of the band's debut, *Definitely Maybe*, was arranged and shot by renowned rock photographer Michael Spencer Jones. The shoot was made more challenging by the fact that the band were drinking, and at one point Liam, true to his self-indulgent nature, decided to simply take off on his motor scooter.

It's common knowledge that
Oasis hail from Manchester,
but where exactly were
the Gallaghers born?

---

a) Longsight

b) Openshaw

c) Denton

THERE'S ELVIS AND ME. I COULDN'T SAY WHICH OF THE TWO IS BEST.

LIAM

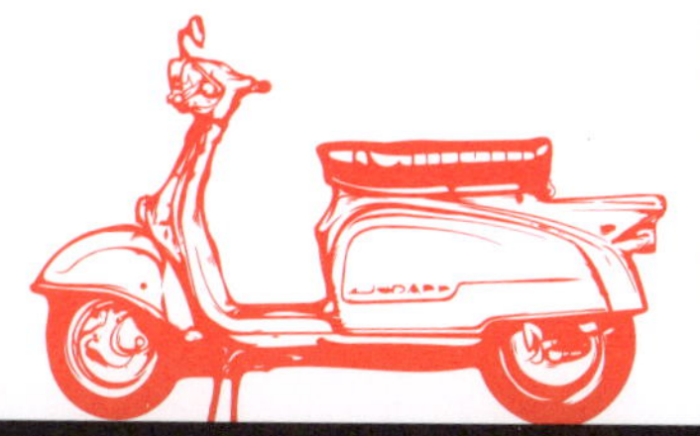

DID YOU KNOW...

The recording of *Definitely Maybe* was far from a straightforward process. The band went through various sessions with two different producers to achieve their signature sound, which actually came courtesy of a third person – Owen Morris – who gave the tracks a bigger, edgier vibe.

Which one of the following
is not an Oasis song?

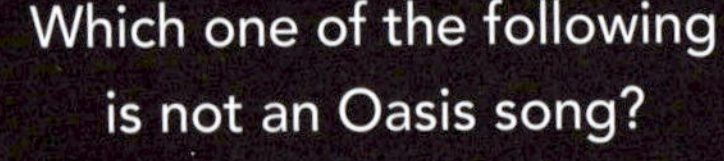

a) "Digsy's Dinner"

b) "Married With Children"

c) "Architect"

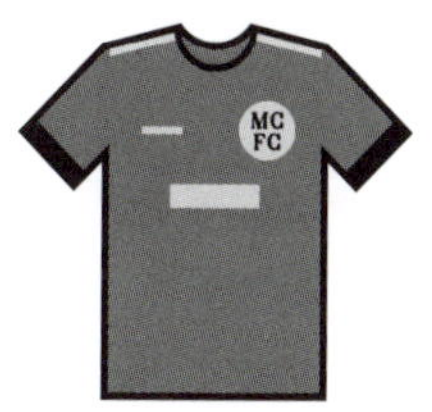

In Britain,
the band reigns
unchallenged as the
most popular act
since the Beatles.

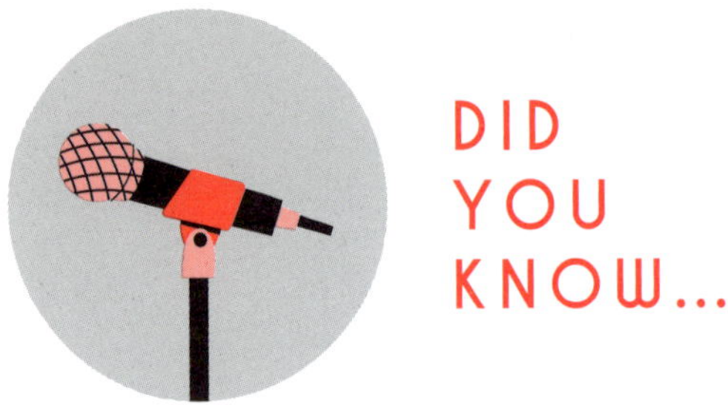

Before becoming one of the most memorable and idiosyncratic frontmen of all time, Liam used to lend a hand to his big brother who had a job as a roadie for the band Inspiral Carpets. It's hard to imagine, but before hitting the big-time, Liam even served as a tax collector!

The Gallagher brothers are nothing if not opinionated, and Noel has been quoted in the press as saying politicians are "idiots". However, back in 1997, he was at a drinks party at 10 Downing Street hosted by…

a) John Major

b) Tony Blair

c) Paddy Ashdown

OASIS WERE THE LAST GREAT, TRADITIONAL ROCK 'N' ROLL

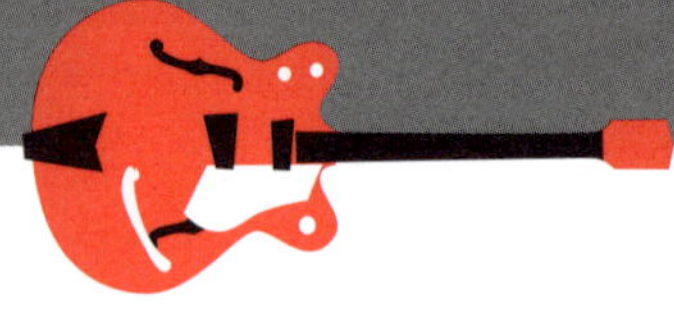

BAND... IF YOU WANTED TO SEE US, YOU HAD TO BE THERE.

NOEL

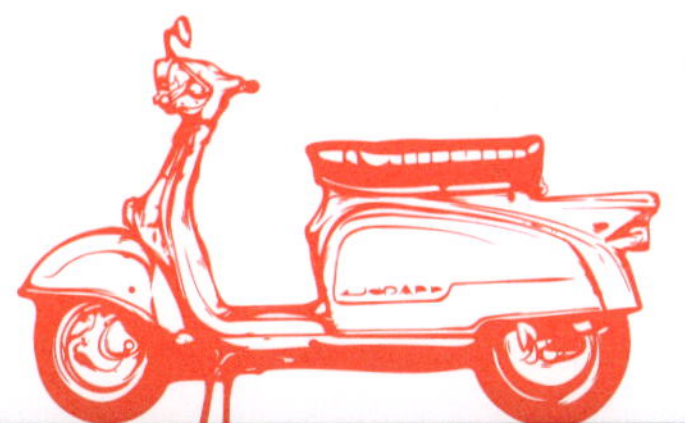

DID YOU KNOW...

Rumour has it that the band's most recognized song, "Wonderwall", was written about an imaginary friend who appears in a time of need. Perhaps that friend is Beatle-shaped, since the title of the track has been linked to a 1968 record by George Harrison named *Wonderwall Music*

In the 1990s, Noel had
two cats whose names were
inspired by one of his regular
vices. The names were…

———

a) Benson and Hedges

b) Vodka and Coke

c) Stella and Carling

IT'S NOT ABOUT THE
MONEY. I DON'T
DRIVE CARS. I DON'T
BUY ROLEXES. BUT
I'VE GOT ENOUGH
PARKAS THAT I
COULD WHIP OUT
AND STILL BLOW
PEOPLE'S MINDS.

LIAM

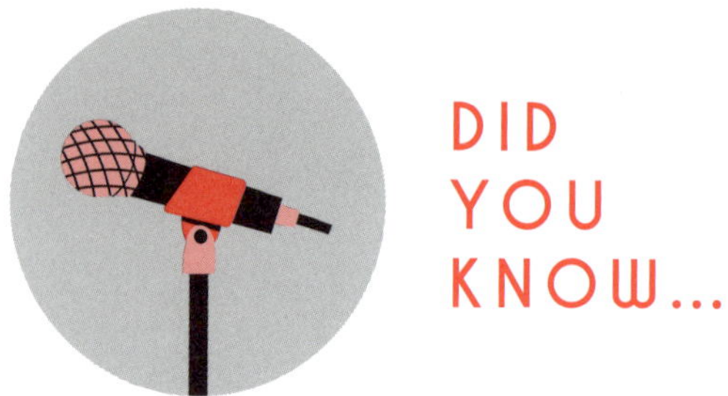

Oasis are no strangers to conflict, and even in their early days they managed to fall foul of copyright law. The Coca-Cola company sued the band for ripping off a company jingle from the 1970s – "I'd Like to Teach the World to Sing (In Perfect Harmony)" – in their second single, "Shakermaker".

Liam and Noel may be the most famous Gallagher brothers from Manchester, but they do in fact have an elder brother. His name is…

____

a) Paul

b) John

c) George

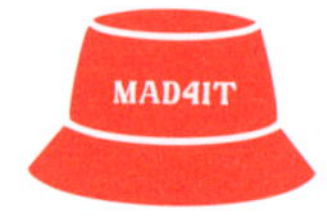

Liam Gallagher
reading his phone
on the toilet would
be more charismatic
and intriguing than
99.9 per cent of the
world's population at
their most enigmatic.

ROBBIE WILLIAMS

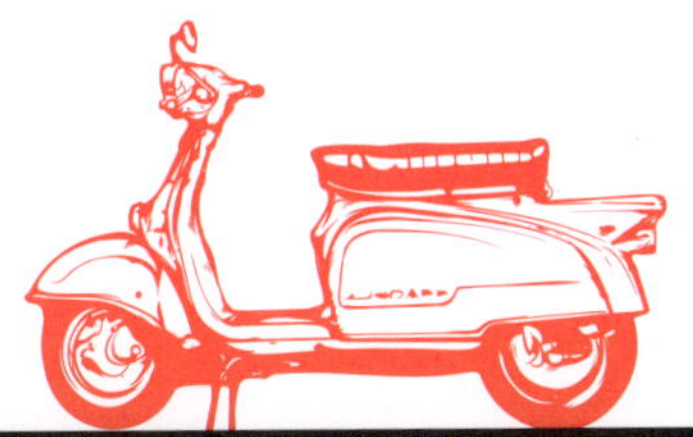

Not only are Oasis mad on football, they also enjoy the occasional bit of cricket. Once, while Noel was at work in a music studio, Liam appeared with a group of mates from the pub. Evidently this irked the eldest brother, and, in true Gallagher fashion, Noel decided to take the direct approach to encouraging his brother to leave – by directly smacking him with a cricket bat!

"Wonderwall" is undoubtedly the band's most recognized song, but it originally had a different title, which was…

———

a) "Northern Lights"

b) "Blind Revelation"

c) "Wishing Stone"

I SUPPOSE I DO
GET SAD, BUT NOT
FOR TOO LONG.
I JUST LOOK

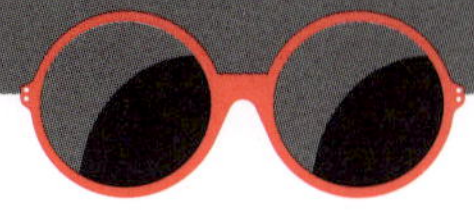

IN THE MIRROR
AND GO, "WHAT
A GOOD-LOOKING
F**K YOU ARE."

LIAM

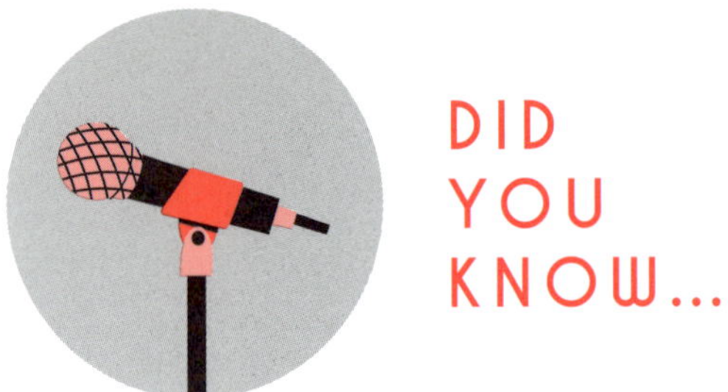

DID YOU KNOW...

The band's first single, "Supersonic", was written and recorded in just one day at the Pink Museum studio in Liverpool. Noel has since said that it's one of his favourite Oasis songs, since, as he put it, "we didn't invest a lot of time in it, in neither mixing it, writing it or f*****g playing it."

It's well known that Noel is the main songwriting force in the band, but there have been several times when he hasn't been involved. *Heathen Chemistry* features the first Oasis single written by Liam – what is it called?

a) "Songbird"

b) "Hung in a Bad Place"

c) "She is Love"

MY FIRST INSTINCT
WHEN I WRITE
SONGS IS NOT A
NEGATIVE ONE. IT'S
SOMETHING POSITIVE.
EVERYTHING I'VE
EVER DONE HAS
SOME FORM OF
HOPE IN IT, I THINK.

NOEL

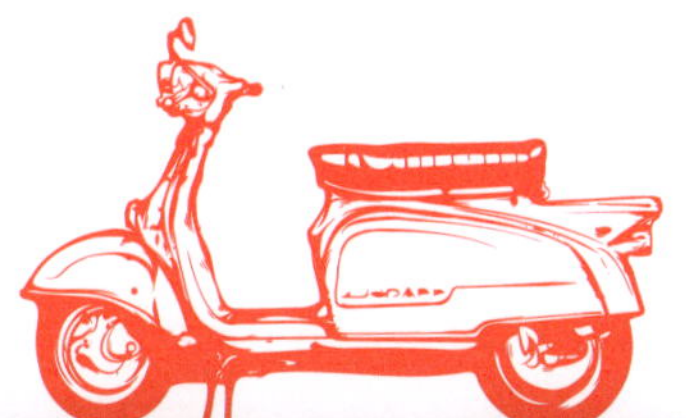

DID
YOU
KNOW...

The track "Slide Away" was written on a 1960 Gibson Les Paul gifted to Noel by Smiths impresario Johnny Marr. Marr himself had acquired the guitar from yet another rock legend: Pete Townshend of the Who.

Which one of the following
is not an Oasis song?

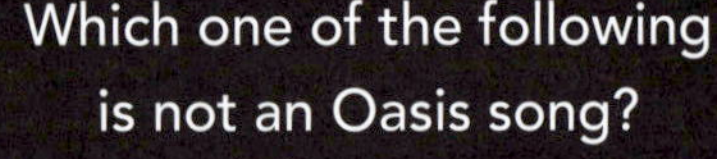

a) "Cast No Shadow"

b) "Rude Awakening"

c) "Hello"

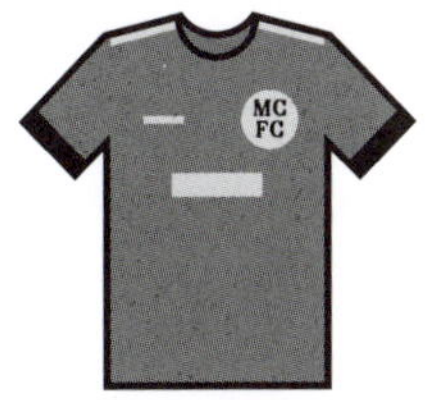

For me, Oasis had
breathed life back
into rock 'n' roll.

GEM

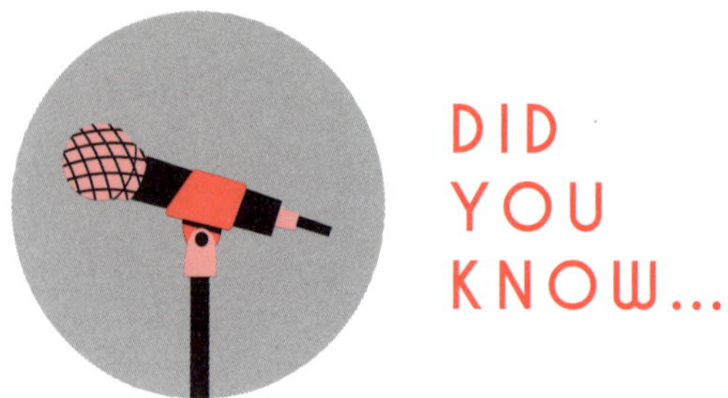

The band's first international concert
was to be held in Amsterdam
in the Netherlands. As bad luck
would have it, during their ferry
crossing to the Dutch city, they
encountered a group of Chelsea
FC fans, whom they proceeded
to fight. As a result, they were
summarily deported upon arrival.

Having got wind that the band enjoyed playing one of their board games while on tour, publisher MB released just 200 Oasis-themed editions of which game?

———

a) *Connect Four*

b) *Guess Who?*

c) *Frustration!*

WE WANT TO PUT KEYBOARDS ON, BUT KEYBOARD PLAYERS DON'T

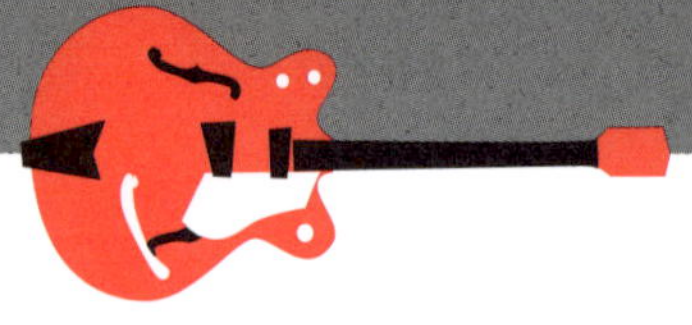

LOOK COOL ONSTAGE... APART FROM ELTON JOHN.

NOEL

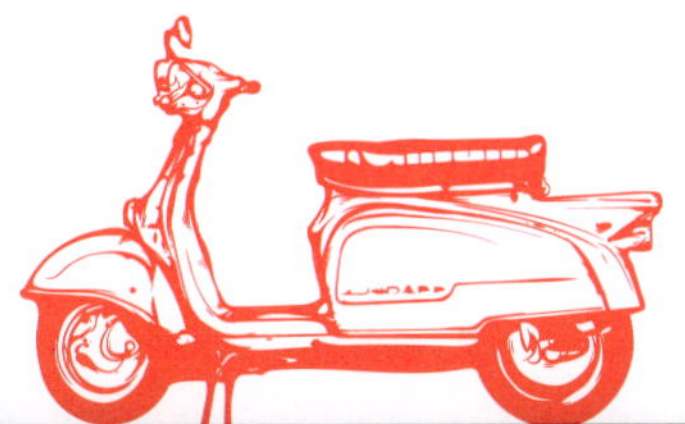

DID YOU KNOW...

In the 1990s, there were plenty of novelty acts and one-hit-wonders making a splash with some pretty questionable music. Arguably, the Mike Flowers Pops were one such act, though they achieved the number-two spot in the UK charts with a cover of none other than "Wonderwall"

By his own admission, original bassist Paul "Guigsy" McGuigan had a simplistic playing style. In the video for "Shakermaker", he can be seen with a Gibson guitar – but what is the model name?

a) Triumph

b) Tribute

c) Thunderbird

THE BEATLES PLAY
GUITARS, WE PLAY
GUITARS. THE BEATLES
GOT HAIR, WE'VE
GOT HAIR. THE
BEATLES GOT ARMS,
WE'VE GOT ARMS.

LIAM

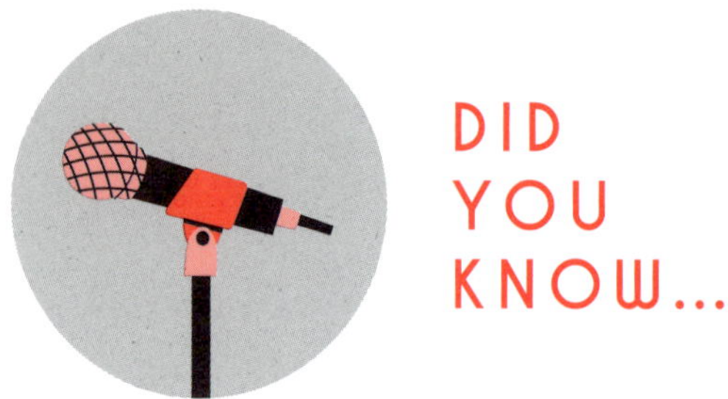

One of the things that makes Oasis songs so memorable is the fact that they're not afraid to repeat themselves. If there's a catchy refrain, you better believe that Liam will be belting it out at least four or five times in the duration of a song. However, in their smash hit, "Live Forever", he sings "maybe" no less than 12 times.

After their initial record label, Creation Records, folded, Oasis decided they might as well start their own label. What was it called?

---

a) Sour Mash Records

b) Big Brother Recordings

c) Charisma Records

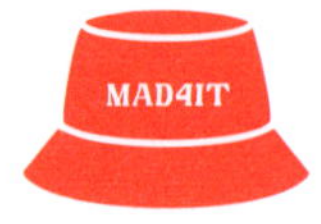

When I first started, I just played up and down the top string of the bass. Come to think of it, that's what I still do now.

GUIGSY

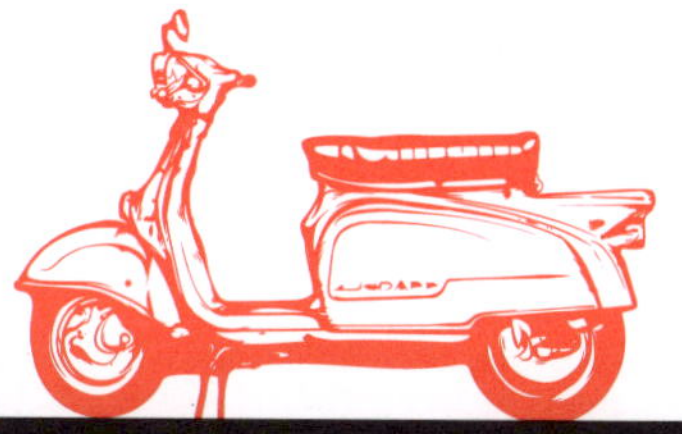

DID YOU KNOW...

True to their habit of incorporating chance influences into their work, the band is reported to have admitted that the reference to "Mr Sifter" in the final verse of "Shakermaker" was included purely because they passed a record shop called Sifters on the way to the studio.

Aside from being the band's longest-serving drummer, Alan White was, at one point, assigned to be Liam's official drinking partner. The pair became so close that they were jokingly referred to as…

a) **Laurel and Hardy**

b) **Batman and Robin**

c) **Bert and Ernie**

I DO ALL THE WORK, SO IT'S ONLY RIGHT THAT I SHOULD

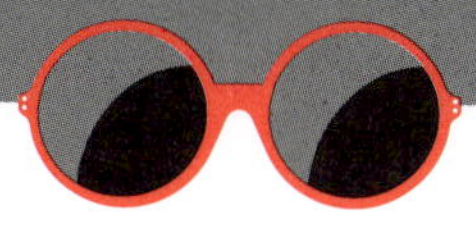

GET THE MOST MONEY. PLUS, I AM THE MOST HANDSOME.

NOEL

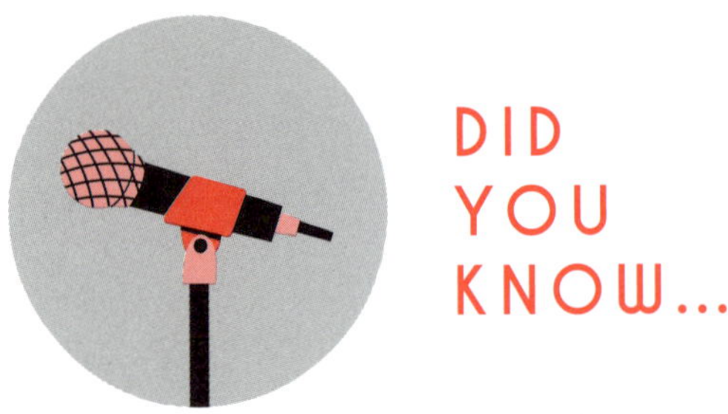

Although Oasis are considered one of the "big four" Britpop bands – along with Suede, Blur and Pulp – the band themselves have never really been happy with that categorization. Liam has been quoted as saying, "I don't think we were a Britpop band, we were just Oasis." Similarly, Noel has explained that Oasis were more like "a punk band with Beatles melodies".

The now-classic Oasis logo was directly inspired by the Decca Records branding from the 1960s. The typeface used is called…

a) Impact

b) Helvetica

c) Arial

IF I LOST MY HAIR, YOU WOULD NEVER SEE ME ON THAT STAGE AGAIN, BECAUSE THERE'S NO PLACE FOR BALDNESS IN ROCK 'N' ROLL.

LIAM

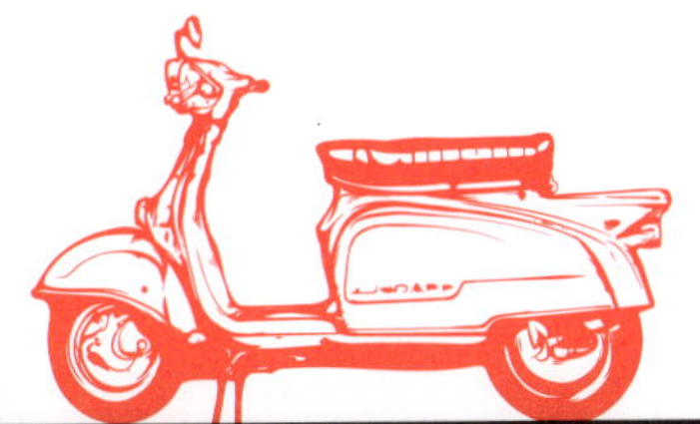

Just like around 10 per cent of the population, Noel is predominantly left-handed. This, in itself, is only vaguely remarkable – but if you consider that he plays guitar with his right hand, it starts to sound a bit more impressive. Instead of seeking out a left-handed guitar or playing upside down like Jimi Hendrix, Noel simply decided to force himself to learn how to play with his non-dominant hand

Liam is known for his bold fashion sense, based somewhat on the classic mod look of the 1960s. However, in the 1990s there was one piece of headgear that he was known for – this was the...

---

a) Bucket hat

b) Beanie

c) Trilby

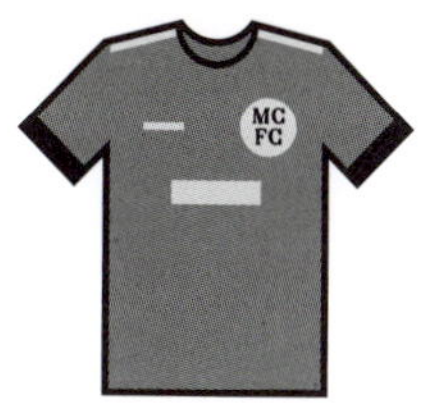

They came to see us... and they were very pleasant... I'd like to see that as a quote: "Oasis are very nice boys."

DAMON ALBARN

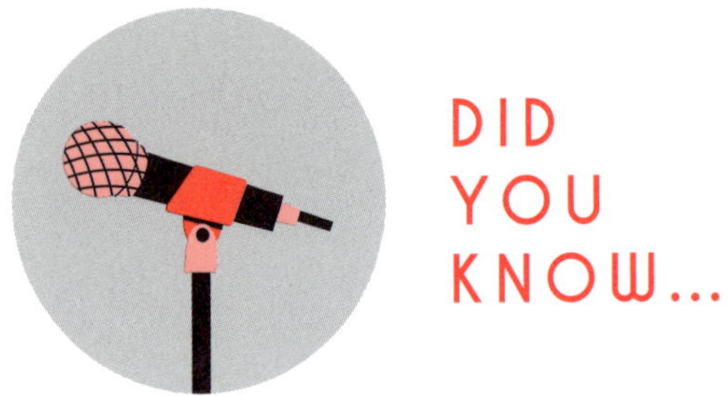

DID
YOU
KNOW...

Liam wasn't always keen on becoming
one of rock's greatest frontmen.
In his youth, he actually thought
music "was for weirdos", until one
fateful day when he received a
blow to the head from a hammer
wielded by an aggressive kid from
a neighbouring school. After he
recovered from the incident, Liam
had a newfound appreciation and
started "hearing music differently".

Which one of the following
is not an Oasis song?

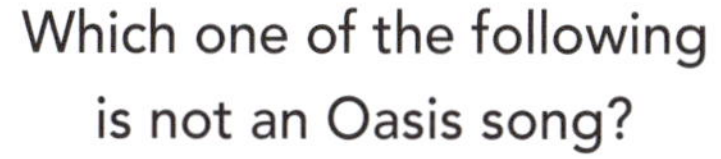

a) "The Girl in the Dirty Shirt"

b) "Magic Pie"

c) "Chasing the Sun"

YOU DON'T HAVE
TO BE GREAT TO
BE SUCCESSFUL.

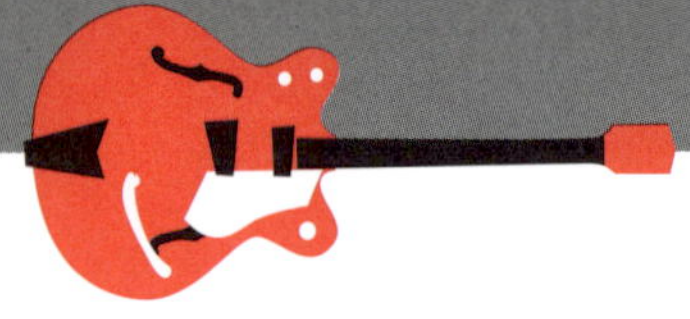

LOOK AT PHIL
COLLINS.

NOEL

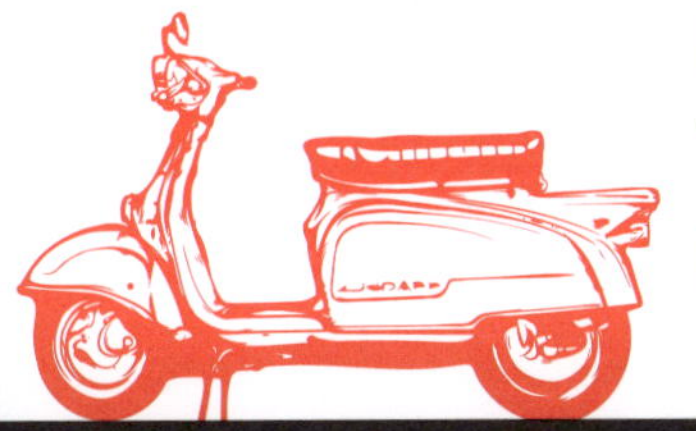

DID YOU KNOW...

It's Liam who's best known for raucous behaviour, but, in his younger days, Noel was a bit of a hell-raiser himself. He has admitted to being expelled from high school at the age of 15. The incident that resulted in his expulsion was one in which he threw a bag of flour down the stairs – and, unfortunately for him, it went over a teacher. Maybe he just wanted someone to "bake along" with?

Oasis recorded at the now-legendary Rockfield Studios in the Wye Valley, Wales. Which of the following 1990s bands did not record at that studio?

a) Coldplay

b) Manic Street Preachers

c) Radiohead

WE DON'T OBSERVE
BANK HOLIDAYS
IN THIS BAND. IT'S
ALL ONE BIG BANK
HOLIDAY, ONE BIG
F*****G DAY OFF.

LIAM

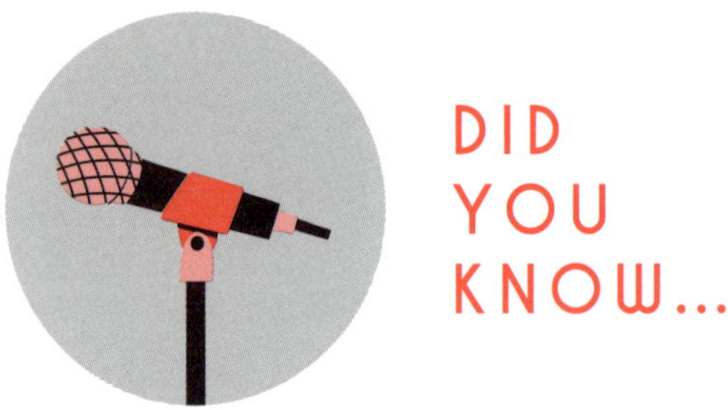

DID YOU KNOW...

The leisure centre that inspired the band's name was based in Swindon, a town in the south-west of England. Despite the impression given by its name, the venue was fully equipped to host music shows, with a concert hall that held up to 3,000 people. Although it attracted various contemporaries, ironically, Oasis never played there. The closest they came was in 2011 when Liam performed there with Beady Eye.

Even while he was the driving creative force in the early days of the band, Noel had outside projects and collaborations. In 1996, he sang on a track with the Chemical Brothers, called…

---

a) "The Devil in Me"

b) "Setting Sun"

c) "Let Forever Be"

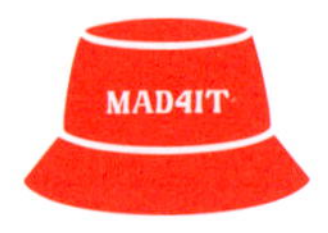

Our attitude is, "Right, we've got all these tunes… We want everyone to hear 'em." We're passionate.

BONEHEAD

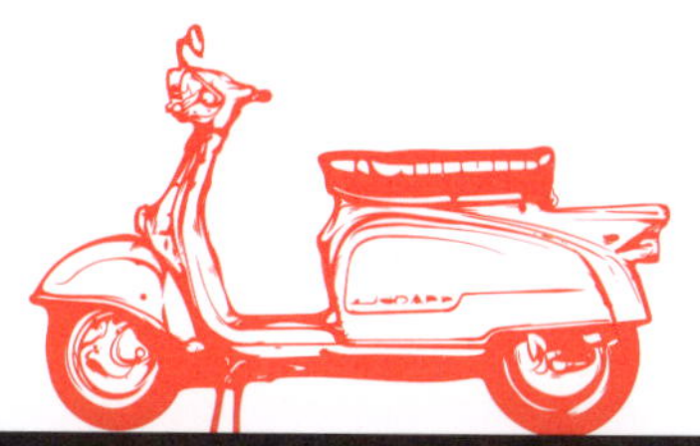

DID YOU KNOW...

The image used on the album cover
for *(What's the Story) Morning Glory?*
was photographed by a graphic
designer by the name of Brian
Cannon. The location is Berwick
Street in the Soho area of London,
and Brian himself features as one of
the people walking along in shot.

Oasis have had phenomenal
success in the UK music charts,
with just as many number-one
singles as number-one albums.
But how many do they have?

———

a) 10

b) 8

c) 5

NOT EVERYONE
CAN SAY, "I'M
GOING TO WRITE
A CLASSIC TODAY."

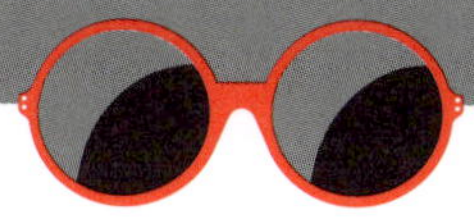

IF THAT WAS
THE CASE, WE'D
ALL BE DOING IT.

LIAM

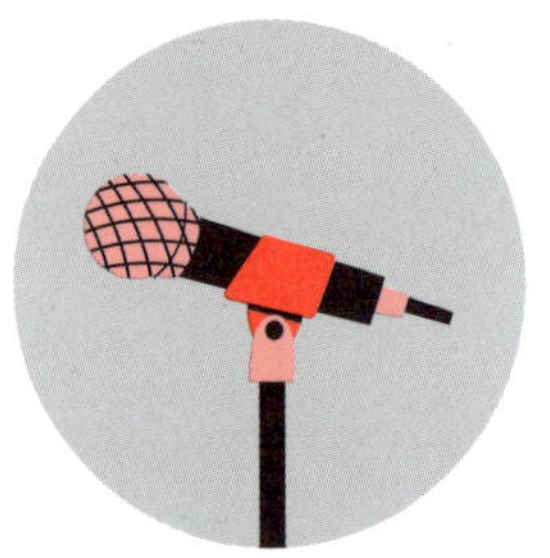

You might think that it's the Gallaghers' egos that drive the idea that Oasis are the best thing since sliced bread, but their record sales back up the claim. Of their seven studio albums, *(What's the Story) Morning Glory?* has sold the most (over 22 million copies), and even their last album, not considered to be their finest work, sold around 2.5 million.

Paul McCartney has had
mixed views on Oasis
over the years, sometimes
complimentary and other
times not. He famously said
that the biggest mistake the
band made was to say that...

---

a) They were the biggest rock
'n' roll band in the world

b) They would outsell the
Rolling Stones

c) They were going to be
bigger than the Beatles

INTERVIEWS ARE
AN OCCUPATIONAL
HAZARD. YOU'RE
SAT IN A ROOM
WITH SOME GUY
FROM STOCKHOLM
WHO YOU'VE
NEVER MET AND
HE'S ASKING YOU
ABOUT YOUR
MUM. IT'S F*****G
PREPOSTEROUS.

NOEL

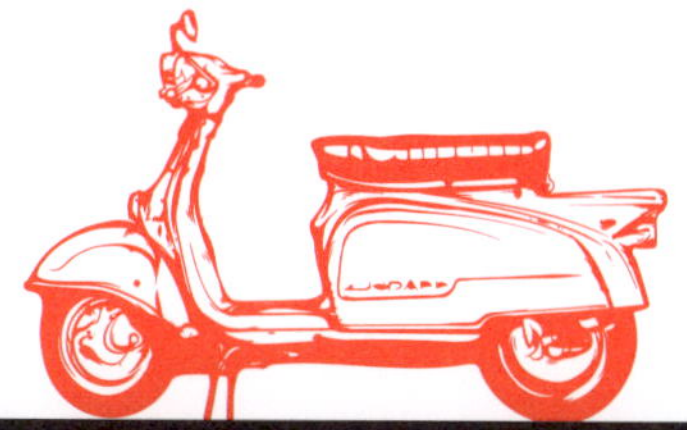

DID YOU KNOW...

The rivalry between Oasis and Blur wasn't just confined to the music charts. In 1996, the bands took part in a friendly football tournament as part of a charity event called Soccer Six. Spectators got what they were hoping for, as Oasis vs Blur was set up for the quarter-final. Liam and Damon Albarn exchanged more than a bit of banter, but despite this the London lads came out on top, beating the Manchester team 2–1.

In 1995, at the height of the antagonism between Oasis and Blur, the rival bands released a single on the same day: Blur's was "Country House", but what was the Oasis track?

---

a) "Wonderwall"

b) "Roll With It"

c) "Don't Look Back in Anger"

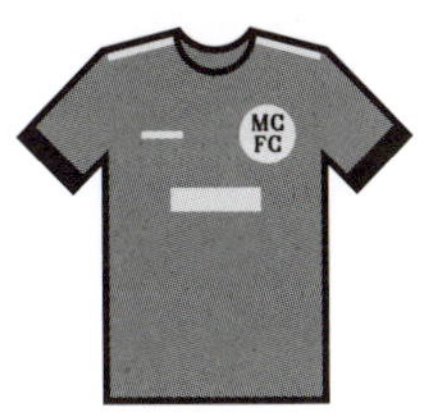

Put Liam in front
of a camera with
Damon next to
him, and Liam…
would rise to
the occasion.

BONEHEAD ON THE
BAND'S RIVALRY
WITH BLUR

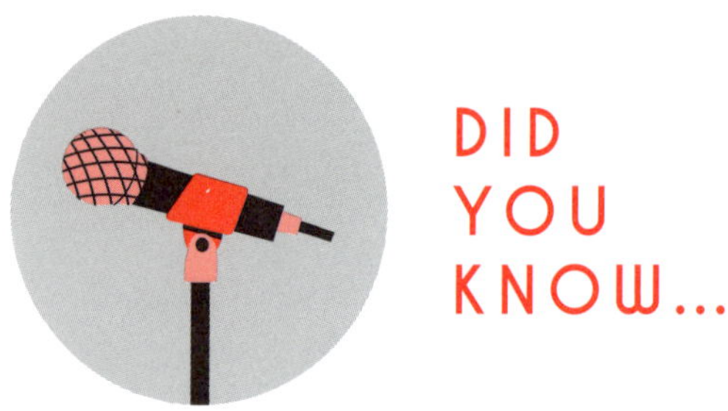

The band's animosity towards Blur showed no sign of abating at the 1996 Brit Awards. Oasis won three awards, while Blur received none. Full of lager and spite, Liam broke into song as he thanked "all the people" in mockery of the "Parklife" chorus. Not his finest moment, but one fitting of his ever-present bravado.

Paul "Guigsy" McGuigan, the band's original bass player, is well known for being obsessive about football. While still performing with Oasis, he wrote a book with Paolo Hewitt called...

———

a) *The Greatest Footballer You Never Saw*

b) *I Think Therefore I Play*

c) *The Damned United*

BEING A LAD IS WHAT I'M ABOUT.

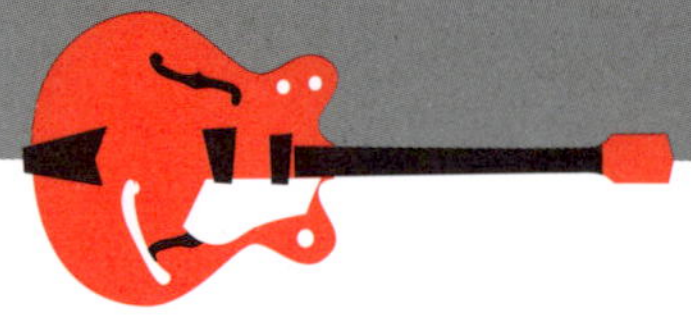

I CAN TELL YOU WHO ISN'T A LAD: ANYONE FROM BLUR.

LIAM

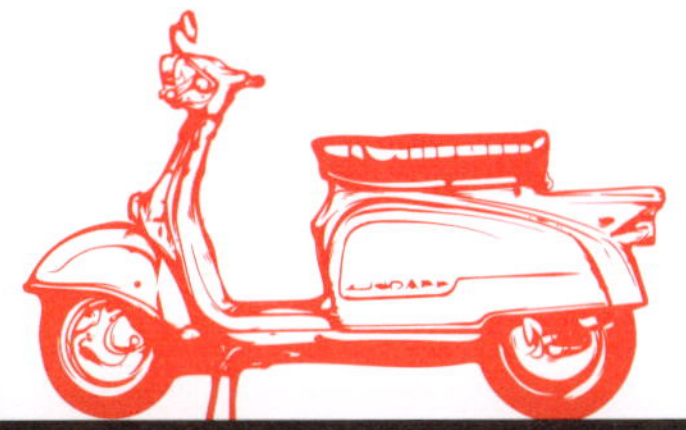

Oasis have never been shy about indulging their baser urges, as the fourth single from their debut, "Cigarettes & Alcohol", shows. The song contains a lyric about a "white line" which, for those who are less familiar with illicit substances, is a reference to cocaine. As such, Noel has claimed that Oasis are the "only band to get a song in the top ten that advocates cocaine use".

Which one of the following
is not an Oasis song?

———

a) "Gas Panic!"

b) "I Can See A Liar"

c) "When I Fall"

I CAN'T MAKE IT
UP WITH NOEL.
BRITPOP WOULD BE
OVER, AND HEAVEN
FORBID THAT WE'D
EVER ADMIT WE'D
ALL GROWN UP!

DAMON ALBARN ON
THE PROSPECT OF
RECONCILING WITH NOEL

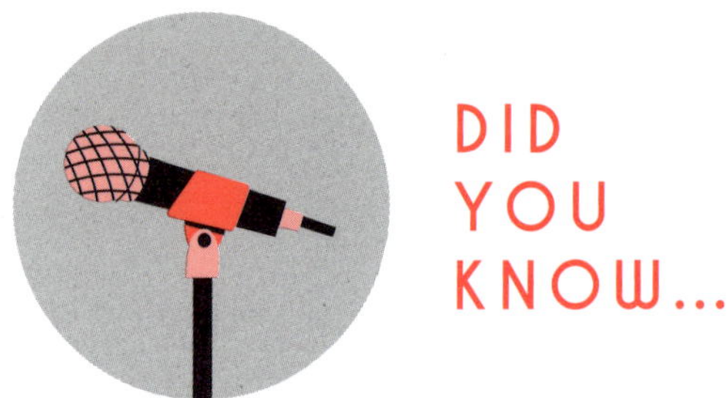

The 2000 album Standing on the Shoulder of Giants is another example of fate intervening with the band's creative direction. The phrase was etched on the outer edge of the £2 coins that were circulating at the time Noel was writing. He liked the sound of it and subsequently wrote it down. Only, he managed to make a slight error in the spelling, omitting the second "s" in "shoulders", which gave the title its grammatical aberration.

There are various "easter eggs" hidden in the shot composed for the cover of *Definitely Maybe*. There are two football legends featured – one from Manchester City and one from Manchester United. Who is the Red Devils' player?

---

a) Denis Law

b) George Best

c) Bobby Charlton

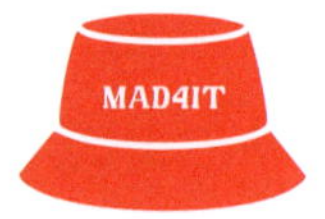

I like Noel outside
the band... But
the geezer that's
in this f*****g
business, he's one
of the biggest c***s
in the universe.

LIAM

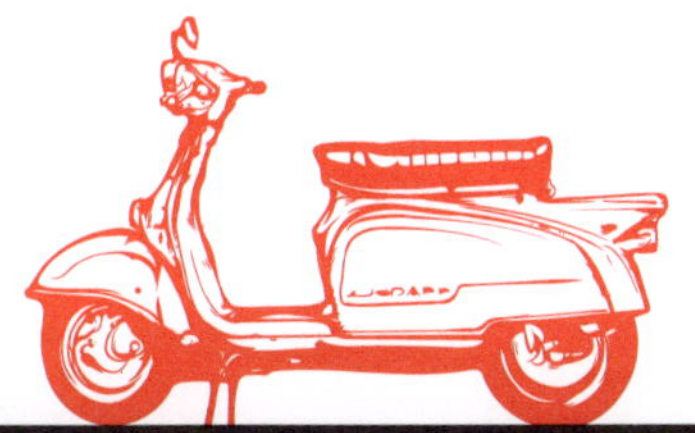

Oasis weren't at war with all of their musical contemporaries. Noel admired grunge pioneer Kurt Cobain greatly, though he wasn't such a fan of the American rocker's bleak outlook. The upbeat lyrics of "Live Forever" are said to be a direct response to Cobain's pessimism – in particular, the song "I Hate Myself and Want to Die"

Even the most casual Oasis fan would struggle to deny that they've had some monumental hits over the years. Can you name their biggest selling song in the UK?

———

a) "Wonderwall"

b) "Don't Look Back in Anger"

c) "D'You Know What I Mean?"

HE'S RUDE,
ARROGANT,
INTIMIDATING
AND LAZY...

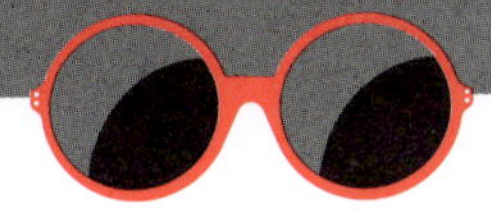

HE'S LIKE A MAN
WITH A FORK IN A
WORLD OF SOUP.

NOEL ON HIS
BROTHER, LIAM

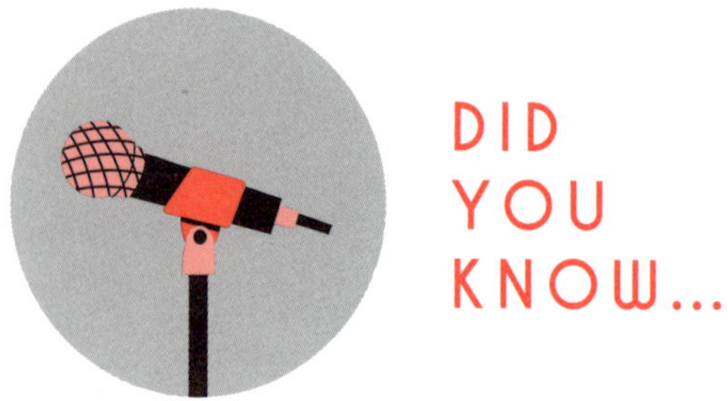

Noel's now-iconic Union Jack guitar was a gift from his then-girlfriend. It's an Epiphone Sheraton – a semi-hollow-body electric guitar, introduced in 1958. The flag paintwork was custom, but it proved to be so impressive that Epiphone started production of the Noel Gallagher Supernova to replicate it.

In 1999, founding member
Paul "Bonehead" Arthurs,
who performed rhythm-guitar
duties on *Definitely Maybe*
and *(What's the Story) Morning
Glory?*, quit the band. Which
album was in the works at
the time of his departure?

---

a) *Heathen Chemistry*

b) *Standing on the
Shoulder of Giants*

c) *Don't Believe the Truth*

PEOPLE SAY
I SEEM VERY
NEGATIVE ABOUT
NEW MUSIC. WELL,
IF SOMEBODY
ASKS ME WHAT I
THINK OF KEANE,
I'LL TELL 'EM. I
DON'T LIKE 'EM.

NOEL

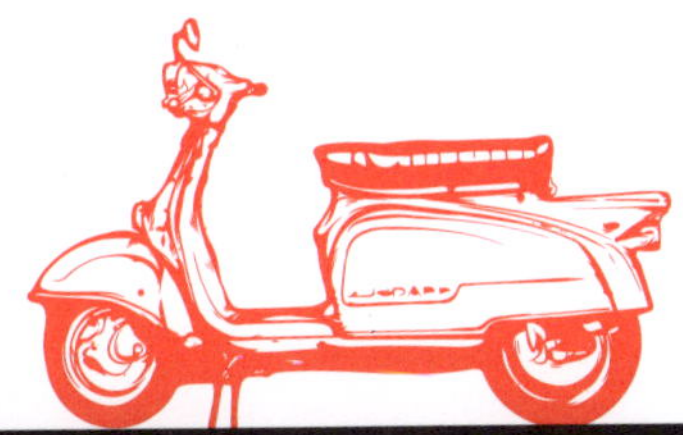

With his mind clearly on career alternatives, Liam set up a clothing brand called Pretty Green just two months before the band split up in 2009. The brand produced mod-inspired clothing fitting of Liam's own evident obsession with the subculture. However, it didn't fare very well, and in November 2020 it was reported that the company owed £16 million to creditors.

Though Oasis are no strangers to accusations of plagiarism themselves, British pop group Girls Aloud were accused of ripping off the melody in "Wonderwall". Which tune was the culprit?

———

a) "Life Got Cold"

b) "Sound of the Underground"

c) "Love Machine"

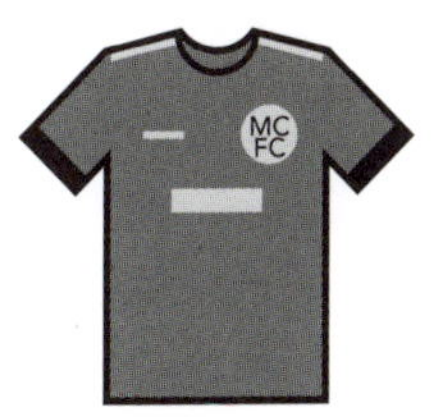

That's the story
of my life, mate;
I'm always
having to go
one louder.

LIAM

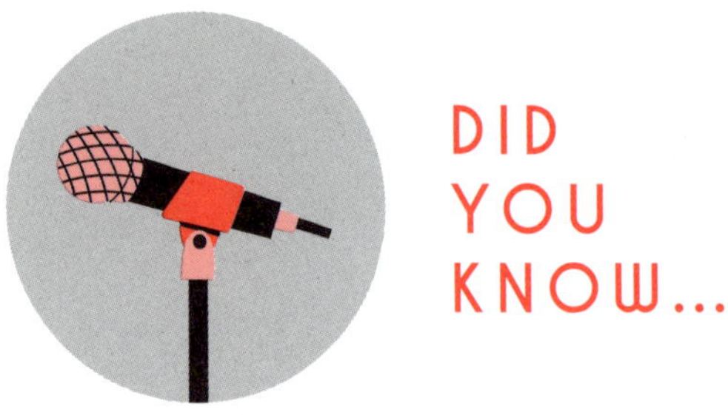

Despite the seemingly interminable animosity between Oasis and Blur, a glimmer of reconciliation appeared in 2017 when Noel performed on the same track with his old mate Damon Albarn. The song was Gorillaz's "We Got the Power".

Oasis have played plenty
of legendary shows, but
they've also turned out some
stinkers. A performance at
an open-air festival in 2004
in the UK was derided by
some as their worst gig ever.
What was the festival?

———

a) Glastonbury

b) Reading

c) T in the Park

F**K RIGHT OFF. I'M NOT HAVING HIM.

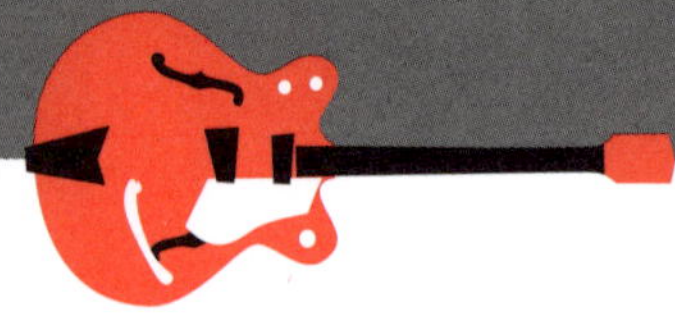

I JUST DON'T LIKE HIS HEAD.

LIAM ON GREEN DAY'S BILLIE JOE ARMSTRONG

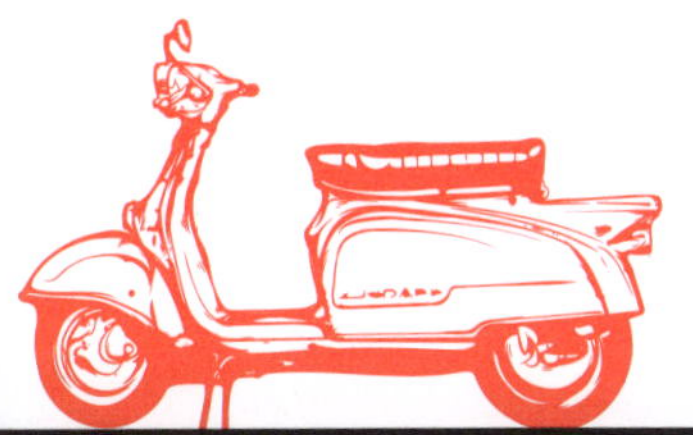

Andy Bell, who joined the band
as an emergency stand-in just
before their 1999 tour, was hired
to play bass. Only, Andy had never
picked one up before! This didn't
faze Liam at all, who reasoned
thusly: "If he can play the guitar,
he can play the f****n' bass."

Though Noel's musical collaborations are numerous, his brother's are less so. He has, however, been identified as performing backing vocals on a track entitled "Come On" by…

---

a) Happy Mondays

b) The Verve

c) The Stone Roses

SINCE THE RISE
OF THE COFFEE
SHOP, CULTURE
HAS DISAPPEARED,
DON'T YOU
THINK? PEOPLE
ARE HORRIFIED
THAT THEY HAVE
TO PAY FOR
MUSIC. MUSIC!
BUT $20 FOR TWO
COFFEES? OH,
ABSOLUTELY.

NOEL

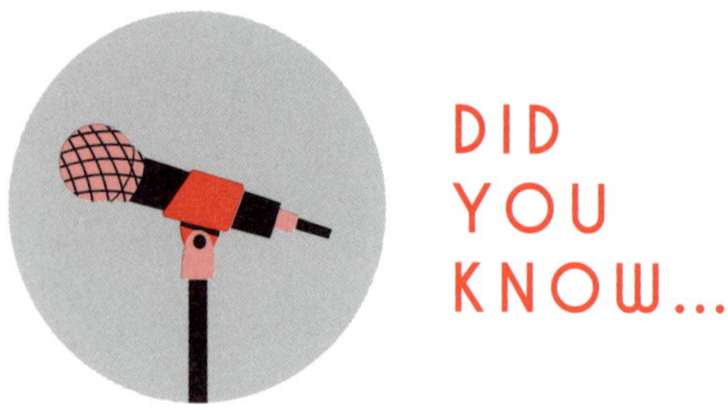

The Beatles influences continued in the band right up until their last album. "I'm Outta Time", on their seventh record *Dig Out Your Soul*, features a sample of John Lennon's voice. The song itself is heavily influenced by the floaty, psychedelic style Lennon and co. were so well known for in their later years.

Which one of the following
is not an Oasis song?

___

a) "The Daily Times"

b) "A Quick Peep"

c) "Born On A Different Cloud"

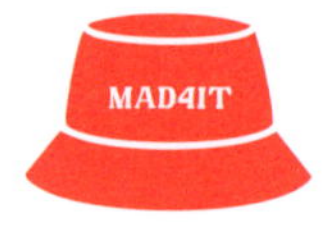

I live for now, not for what happens after I die. If I die and there's something afterwards, I'm going to hell, not heaven.

LIAM

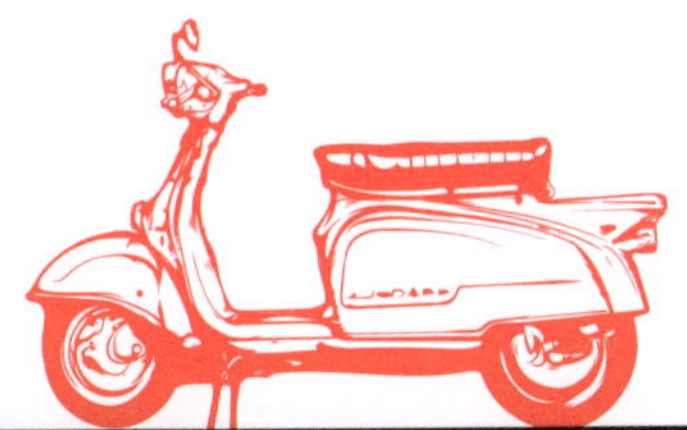

DID YOU KNOW...

Tony McCarroll, the band's original drummer, was dismissed in 1995. Considering the projected success of Oasis, this evidently didn't sit too well with Tony, and in 1999 he hired a solicitor to sue the band for £18 million (his calculated share in the profits of the five-album deal signed while he was in place). However, he accepted an out-of-court settlement of a mere £550,000.

While Oasis took inspiration from many legendary bands that came before them, they too have inspired some remarkable acts. Which of the following bands has not cited an influence?

a) Arctic Monkeys

b) The Killers

c) The Strokes

THERE IS NO GOD.

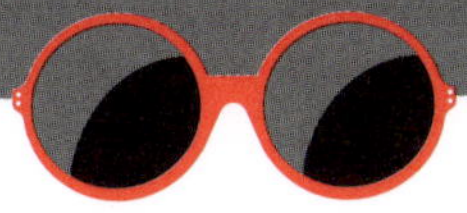

NOEL ON LEARNING
WESTLIFE HAD BEATEN
OASIS, U2 AND THE
BEATLES IN AN ALBUM-
CHART BATTLE IN
NOVEMBER 2006

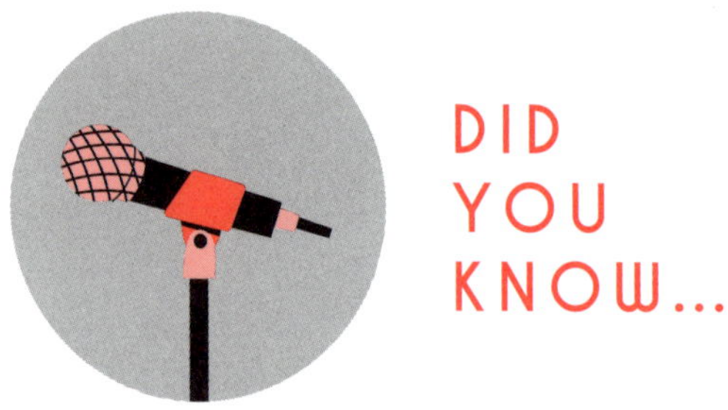

DID YOU KNOW...

While many bands struggle to reach the heights of their debut record with their second release, for Oasis it was more of a third-album fumble. *Be Here Now* was received warmly by the music press and by fans, but, in retrospect, Noel reached the eventual opinion that it was really little more than "the sound of five men in the studio, on coke, not giving a f**k".

Even though "Wonderwall"
is considered to be the
quintessential Oasis song,
the music video – directed
by Nigel Dick – does not
feature original member Paul
McGuigan. This is because
Guigsy had quit the band,
reportedly due to…

a) A raging argument

b) Nervous exhaustion

c) Having to attend rehab

NAME ONE ROCK
STAR IN BRITAIN
APART FROM A
MEMBER OF OASIS.
NAME ONE!

LIAM

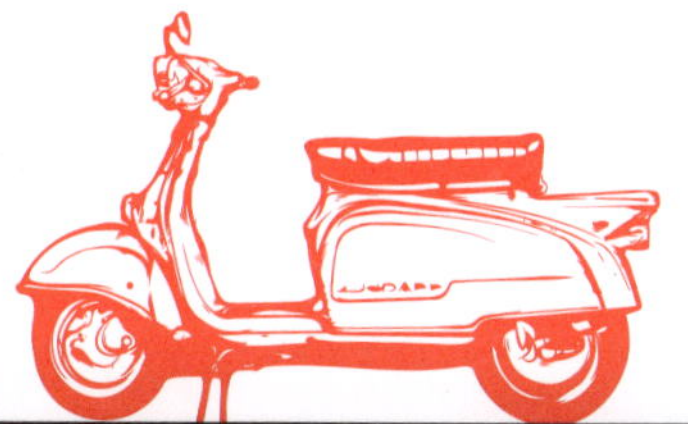

DID YOU KNOW...

Not only is Noel the main creative force behind Oasis, he also marshals most of the business savvy. He owns all of the rights to the band's music – a fact that Liam found out the hard way, having been denied permission to use various songs in a documentary he was attached to

Beatles connections abound throughout the history of Oasis, but during the recording of the 2005 album *Don't Believe the Truth* the son of one of the Fab Four – Zak Starkey – played drums. Which Beatle is Zak's father?

---

a) Paul

b) George

c) Ringo

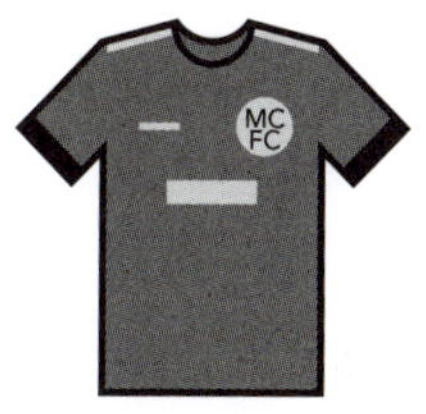

If you're not in it
to be bigger than
the Beatles, it's
just a hobby.

NOEL

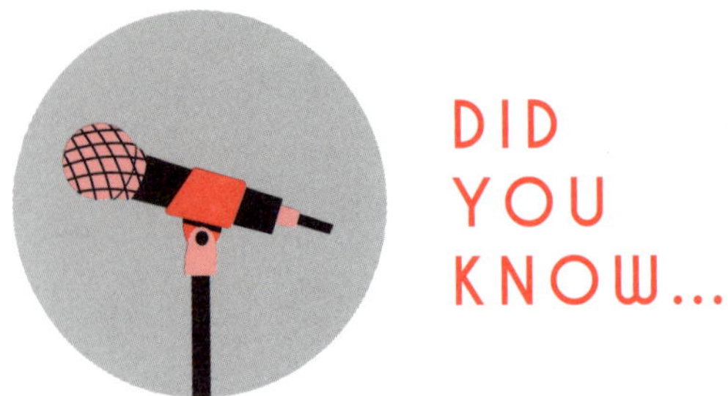

The track "Columbia", from *Definitely Maybe*, is titled after a hotel of the same name near Hyde Park in London. The band had been staying there and, after indulging in some classic rock 'n' roll behaviour, were subsequently banned.

Liam claims to have never held a microphone directly in his life, insisting that his laid-back singing stance is so he can…

______

a) Get more power from his voice

b) Avoid straining himself while singing

c) Reduce his exposure to foldback noise

I HAVE GOT A BIT OF AN ISSUE WITH CARDIGANS.

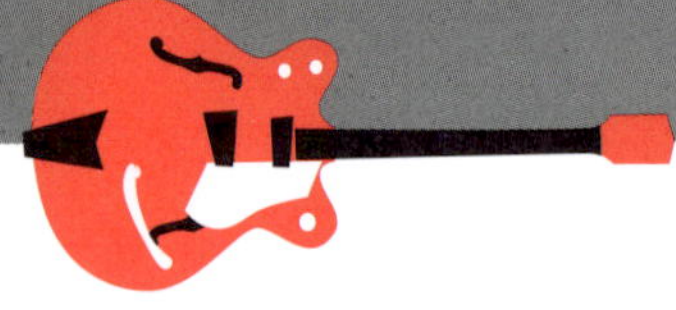

THEY'RE S**T, AREN'T THEY?

LIAM

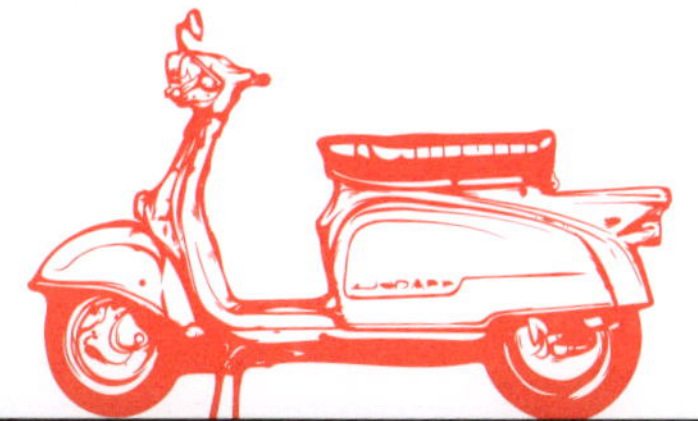

DID YOU KNOW...

True to the live-fast, laissez-faire image Oasis have projected since their debut, Noel once explained that he had quite a bit of chemical assistance during the early days. He has been quoted as saying: "I was on drugs before I was even in a band. The whole of the first three albums were written on drugs. That's why they're so good."

In 2007, a documentary film directed by Baillie Walsh was released. It covered the exploits of the band's *Don't Believe the Truth* tour – but what was the film called?

————

a) *Lord Don't Slow Me Down*

b) *The Meaning of Soul*

c) *Keep the Dream Alive*

GREAT MUSIC IS
IN THE EAR OF
THE BEHOLDER.

NOEL

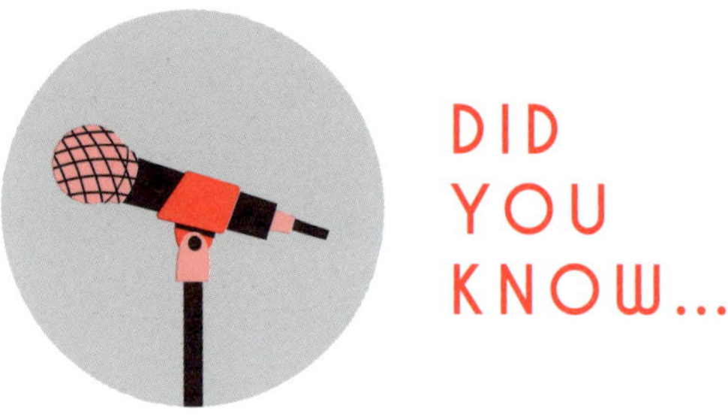

DID YOU KNOW...

Anyone who says there's only one Oasis might be due for a rethink. In 2023, AISIS (pronounced A-I-SIS) released a full-length Oasis-style album using AI vocals. The band behind the music are called Breezer, and the record was their attempt to recreate the Mancunian magic using real players and a computer-generated Gallagher voice. Reportedly, Liam was impressed with the results!

The band's legendary performance at Knebworth in 1996 was a record-breaking event in numerous ways. Of the reported 7,000 people on the guestlist, a number of VIPs were awarded a pair of Oasis-branded...

a) Binoculars

b) Briefs

c) Trainers

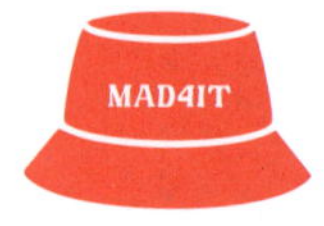

At Knebworth,
I thought we
were doing one
night and we
were doing two...
I had to go and
do it again. That
was heavy.

LIAM

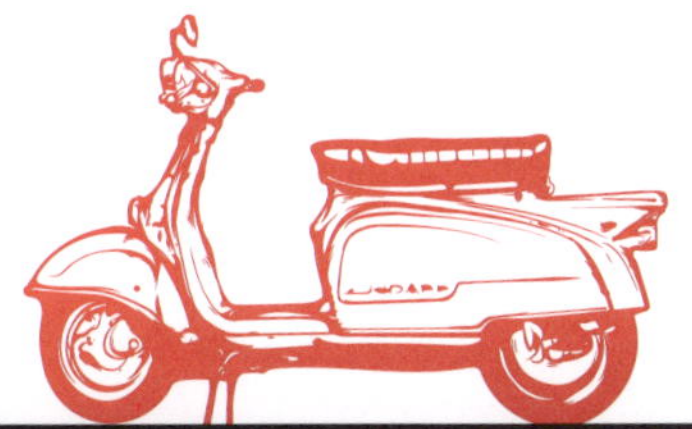

DID YOU KNOW...

Perhaps in an effort to embody the carefree attitude suggested in the title of the song, Noel turned up to the video shoot for "Whatever" still drunk from the previous night's session. Evidently, he managed to hold it together, but he later admitted that he was "s**tfaced" and had woken up in a bus shelter that morning.

Which one of the following
is not an Oasis song?

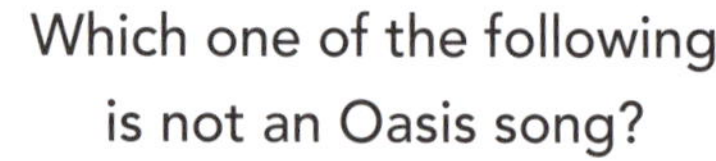

a) "Mucky Fingers"

b) "A Bell Will Ring"

c) "Kaleidoscope"

DON'T MUCH LIKE
"WONDERWALL",
BUT THE EFFECT

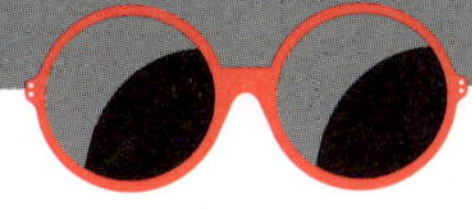

THAT SONG HAS
ON PEOPLE, I
CAN'T DENY IT.

NOEL

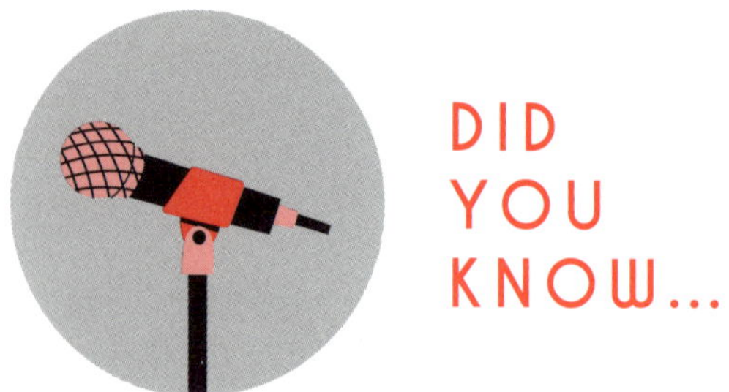

DID YOU KNOW...

It took 3,000 crew members
to pull off the Knebworth gig,
which featured no less than
11 speaker towers. Britannia
Row were the company
behind the enormous
sound that was achieved.

At the time of writing, Oasis have released seven studio albums. Most will remember their first two – *Definitely Maybe* and *(What's the Story) Morning Glory?* – but what was their seventh (released in 2008) called?

---

a) *Dig Out Your Soul*

b) *Heathen Chemistry*

c) *Don't Believe the Truth*

I'M LIKE A LITTLE
BUMPER CAR – I
KEEP BUMPING
INTO QUESTIONS
AND ANSWERS,
AND IT'S A TOP
BUZZ, MAN.

LIAM

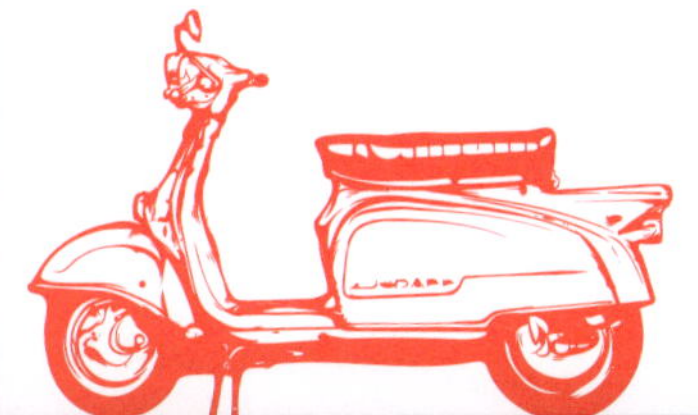

Of course, if one were to ask Noel or Liam, the answer to the question of whether Oasis are the biggest band in the world would be met with an emphatic "yes". And they would be right! At the time of writing, they've sold over 75 million records and, as such, are one of the bestselling bands of all time

Noel's low-key, bittersweet anthem "Half the World Away", which appeared on the compilation album *The Masterplan*, was used as the theme song to which British sitcom?

———

a) **Gavin & Stacey**

b) *Early Doors*

c) *The Royle Family*

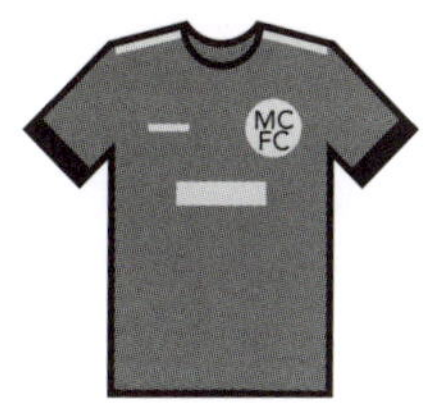

The 1990s
was not the
beginning... it
was the end...
We were the
last rock stars.

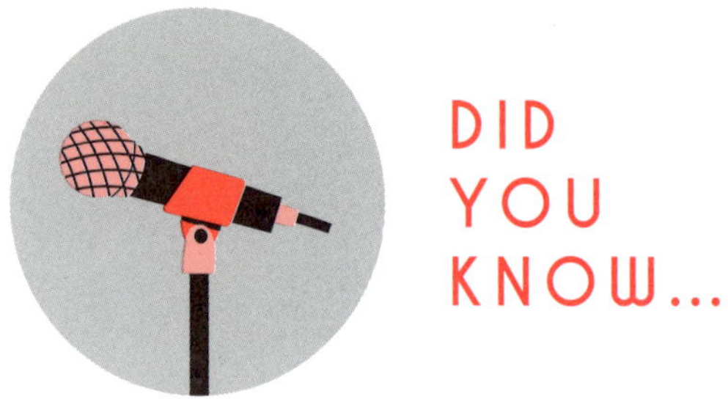

The scooter that Liam kept escaping on during the photo shoot for *Definitely Maybe* ended up featuring on the cover of their third album, *Be Here Now*. The other vehicle in the frame was a 1972 Rolls-Royce Silver Shadow which was half-submerged in water in the swimming pool.

Oasis split up in August 2009, with Noel stating that he "simply could not go on working with Liam a day longer". What French music festival were they due to play at the time?

———

a) Rock en Seine

b) Vieilles Charrues

c) Le Cabaret Vert

ANYONE TOUGH ENOUGH TO TAKE US

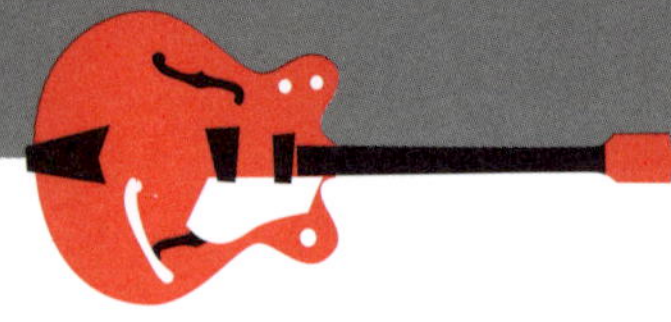

OFF THIS STAGE CAN COME UP NOW!

LIAM AT THE BRIT AWARDS

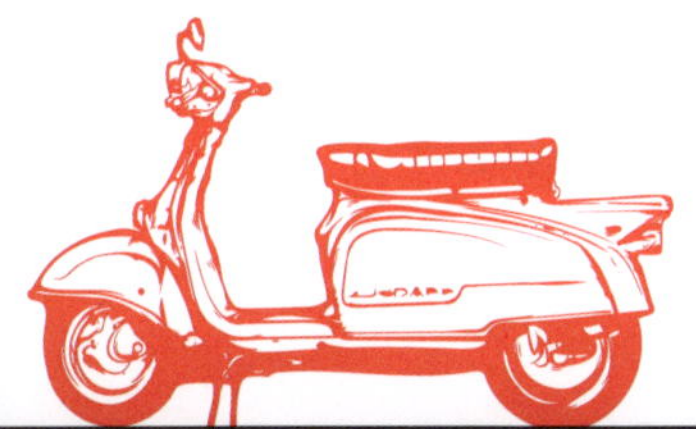

Not only was *Standing on the Shoulder of Giants* a departure from Oasis's earlier sound, it was also recorded without founding members Bonehead and Guigsy. Even the cover wasn't in keeping with their classic style, featuring a generic-looking cityscape and a jarringly modern, reworked logo.

In the late 2000s, Noel
had taken to documenting
the band's tour exploits
in an online blog. What
was it called?

———

a) *Tales from the Middle
of Nowhere*

b) *Notes from the Road*

c) *Digging Out My Soul*

I'M USED TO PEOPLE
BEING A MILE AWAY.
THAT SUITS ME.
IT'S MORE NERVE-
WRACKING PLAYING
IN FRONT OF PEOPLE
WHO ARE TWO FEET
AWAY FROM ME.

NOEL

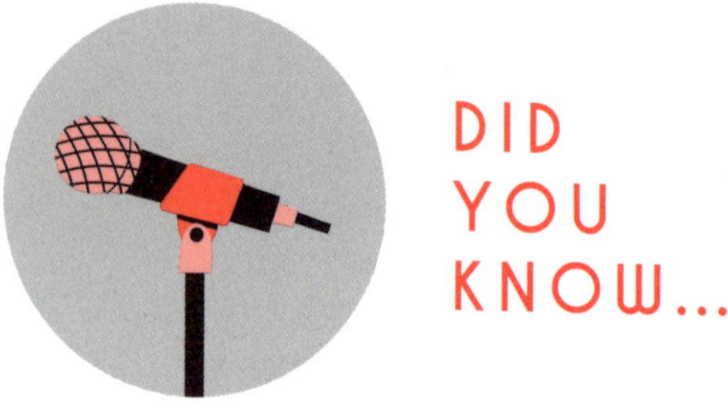

In 2024, Oasis were nominated for induction into the Rock & Roll Hall of Fame. They ultimately didn't make the cut, but it was fairly obvious that Liam at least was not particularly bothered. He commented that the Hall was "full of bumboclaats" and that he didn't need "some w**k award [given] by some geriatric in a cowboy hat".

Oasis have enjoyed huge commercial success and have been recognized in various awards ceremonies. At the 2010 Brit Awards, which album was named "Best British Album of 30 Years"?

---

a) *(What's the Story) Morning Glory?*

b) *Definitely Maybe*

c) *Be Here Now*

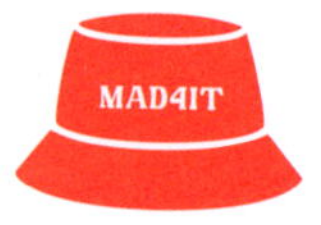

I've mellowed,
but not in the
sense of liking
Radiohead
or Coldplay.

LIAM ON
GETTING OLDER

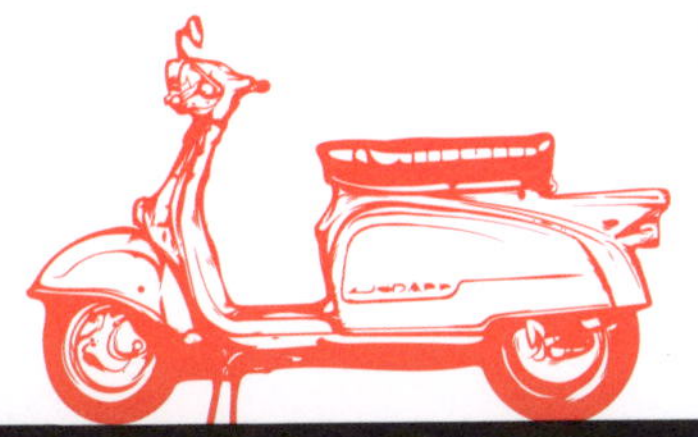

Liam's short-lived, post-break-up project, Beady Eye, reunited former Oasis members Gem Archer and Andy Bell. They released two studio albums – *Different Gear, Still Speeding* (2011) and *BE* (2013) – but only managed one

Which one of the following
is not an Oasis song?

———

a) "Waiting For The Rapture"

b) "Thunderstorms Ahead"

c) "The Turning"

I LIKE TO THINK I KEEP IT REAL. LIAM KEEPS IT SURREAL,

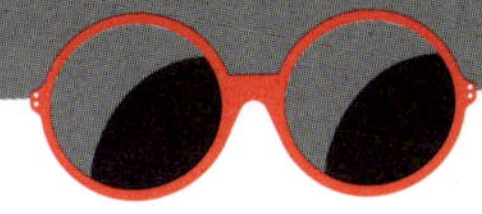

AND SOMEWHERE BETWEEN THE TWO WE GET ON ALL RIGHT.

NOEL

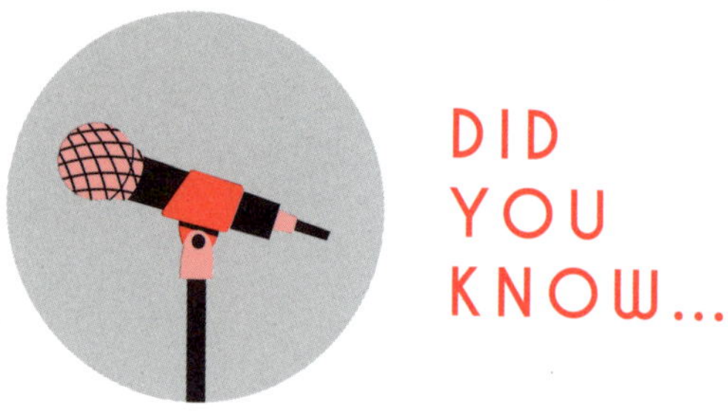

Noel's post-break-up project, Noel Gallagher's High Flying Birds, fared much better than little brother Liam's efforts. At the time of writing, the band had four albums under its belt – *Noel Gallagher's High Flying Birds* (2011), *Chasing Yesterday* (2015), *Who Built the Moon?* (2017) and *Council Skies* (2023) – the first of which debuted at number one in the UK Albums Chart.

Which music industry executive originally signed Oasis?

---

a) Alan McGee

b) Chris Blackwell

c) Richard Branson

NO DOUBT HE'D
HAVE A FANTASTIC
ONE-LINER ABOUT
WHAT A BUNCH
OF F*****G
KNOBHEADS
WE ARE.

DAMON ALBARN ON
LIAM'S IMAGINED
RESPONSE TO THE
GORILLAZ COLLAB
WITH NOEL

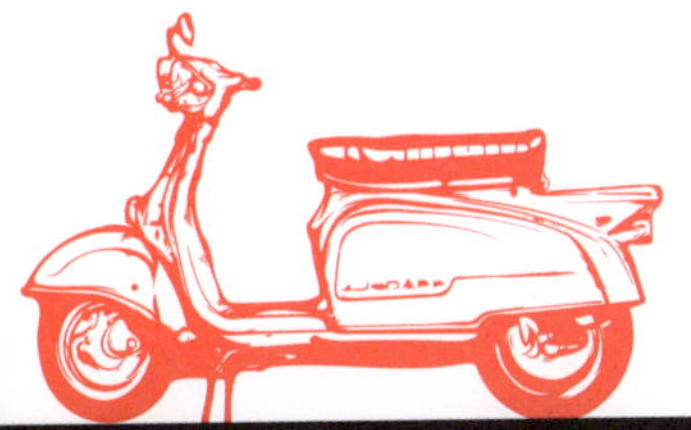

"Champagne Supernova", from the album *(What's the Story) Morning Glory?*, is celebrated as one of the band's best songs. However, not everyone in the press was convinced. Noel recalled one writer who said that it could be a classic if it weren't for nonsensical lyrics like "Slowly walking down the hall, faster than a cannonball". Noel reacted by saying that even he "hasn't got a clue" what it means!

In 1996, Liam pulled out of performing for an episode of *MTV Unplugged*. What did he do instead?

---

a) Went to the pub

b) Left to go and eat pizza

c) Watched from the balcony at the venue and heckled his brother

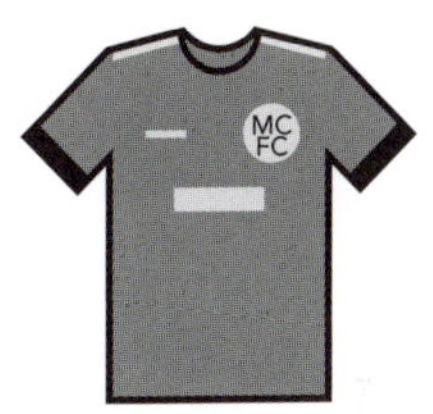

It was only when
I got on tour that
I was thinking,
"It doesn't f*****g
stand up."

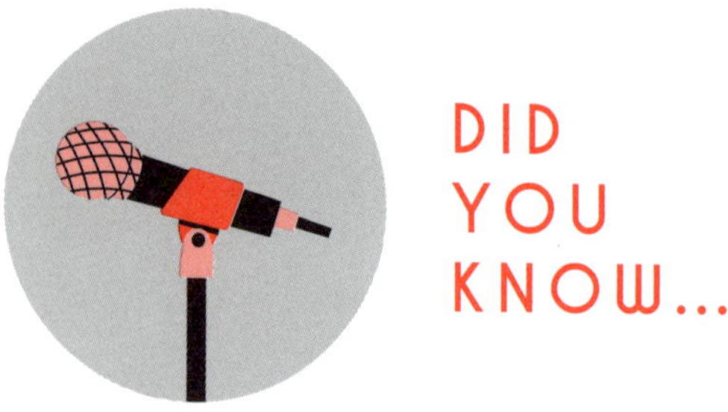

Heathen Chemistry, the band's fifth studio release, was reported to have been the victim of an internet leak – that is, the songs had made it onto the internet and had been shared before the official release date. This became evident at a show in Las Vegas before the album's release, where somehow the audience were able to sing along to the new material.

Paul Arthurs, one of the co-founders of the band, is known affectionately as "Bonehead". How did he get the name?

a) He was known for being a bit dim

b) His parents used to insist he get short haircuts as a child

c) He was into dinosaurs

THE GUNS HAVE FALLEN SILENT. THE STARS HAVE ALIGNED.

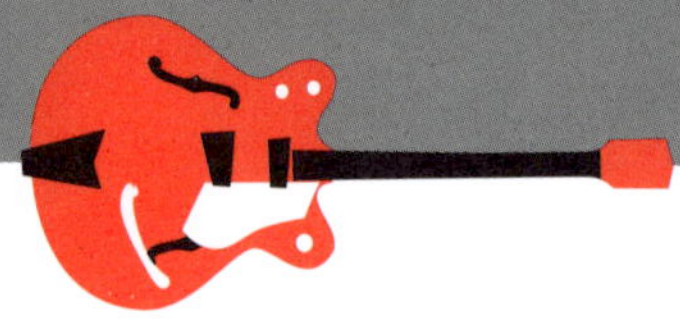

THE GREAT WAIT IS OVER. COME SEE. IT WILL NOT BE TELEVISED.

OASIS REUNION ANNOUNCEMENT IN 2024

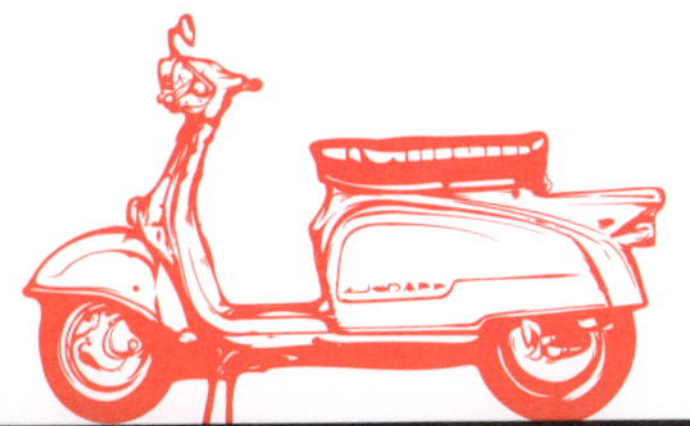

DID YOU KNOW...

Oasis aren't famous for their collaborations, but they were sufficiently convinced by the talents of one Johnny Depp to let him loose on slide guitar for "Fade In-Out". That is, Noel was reportedly too drunk to play, so Depp did the honours.

Oasis's phenomenal success has resulted in them achieving numerous Guinness World Records. Which of the following have they not won?

a) Longest Top-10 UK Chart Run by a Group

b) Most Successful Act in the UK Between the Years 1995 and 2005

c) Most Consecutive UK Number Ones in the 1990s

BEING ME IS THE
BEST F*****G GIG
IN THE WORLD.

LIAM

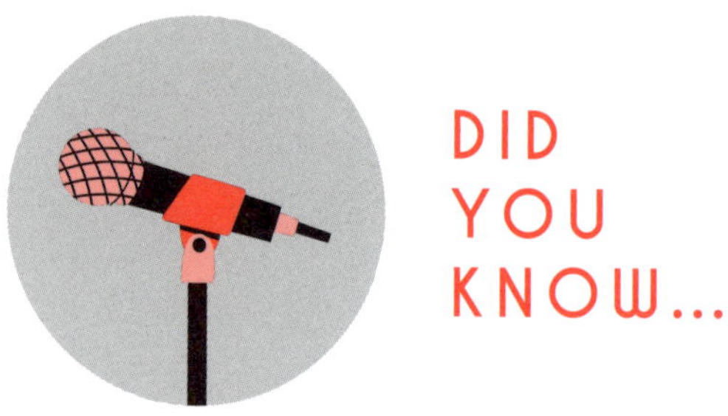

Always one to recognize and celebrate his northern connections, Noel has gone on record to say that the song "Cast No Shadow" – from *(What's The Story) Morning Glory?* – was written for Richard Ashcroft of the Verve. Noel considers the lyrics to be "the best words I ever wrote" and Ashcroft has been quoted as saying the track is "a great honour".

At their legendary
Knebworth gig, which of
the following bands did
not perform as support?

---

a) The Charlatans

b) The Prodigy

c) Pulp

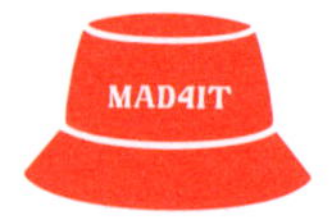

Oasis can't be summed up in one word. I could do a sentence: Boys from council estate made it very, very big.

NOEL

FINAL WORD

Now that you've read this book, you're primed and ready for whatever Oasis has in store next – another blockbuster album, another sold-out world tour or another blazing backstage bust-up. You've absorbed a little bit of the northern soul that has driven the band to their legendary status, and you can take it with you along all the winding roads you have to walk on your own incredible journey.

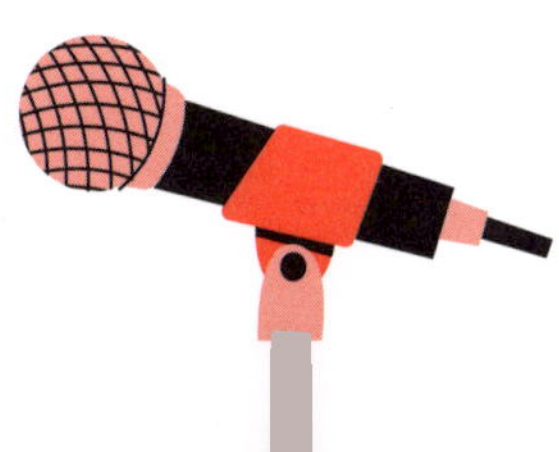

ANSWERS

8. b	47. b
11. c	50. c
14. a	53. b
17. a	56. a
20. c	59. c
23. b	62. c
26. a	65. b
29. a	68. b
32. c	71. c
35. a	74. b
38. b	77. a
41. c	80. c
44. a	83. b

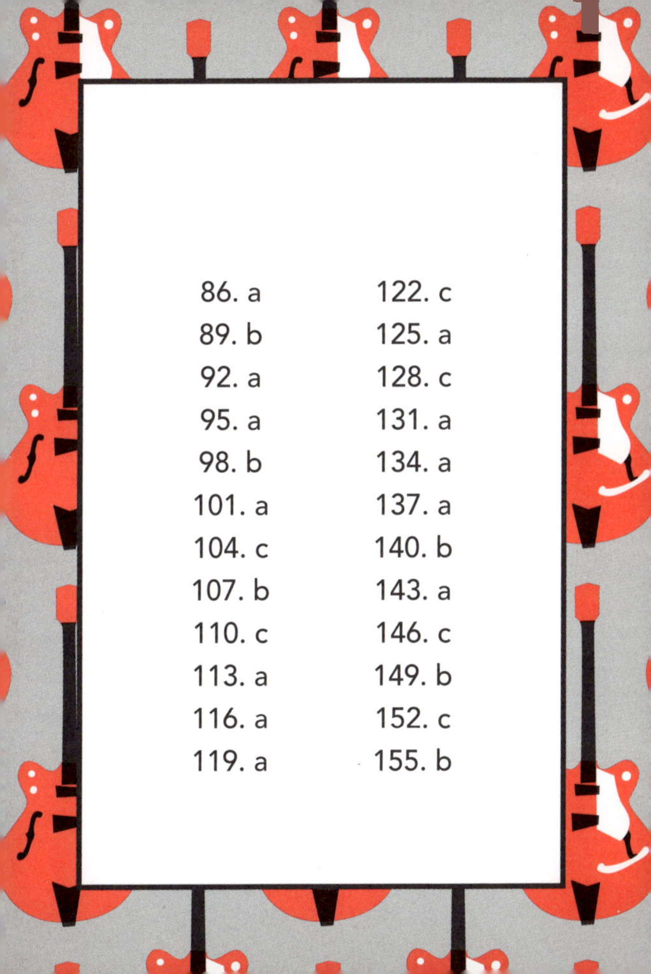

86. a
89. b
92. a
95. a
98. b
101. a
104. c
107. b
110. c
113. a
116. a
119. a
122. c
125. a
128. c
131. a
134. a
137. a
140. b
143. a
146. c
149. b
152. c
155. b

Have you enjoyed this book?
If so, find us on Facebook at
Summersdale Publishers, on
Twitter/X at **@Summersdale**
and on Instagram and TikTok at
@summersdalebooks and get in
touch. We'd love to hear from you!

www.summersdale.com

IMAGE CREDITS

Cover – guitar © Birth Brand/Shutterstock.com;
flag © Globe Turner/Shutterstock.com; moped ©
Podessto/Shutterstock.com; p.3 and throughout
© Lavrentsov Dmitrii/Shutterstock.com; p.5
and throughout © Tartila/Shutterstock.com; p.6
and throughout © bus109/Shutterstock.com;
p.7 and throughout © Podessto/Shutterstock.
com; p.8 and throughout © Globe Turner/
Shutterstock.com; p.11 and throughout © Ann
Precious/Shutterstock.com; p.12 and throughout
© Sugar Stock/Shutterstock.com; p.21 and
throughout © tomambroz/Shutterstock.com